WRITTEN AND ILLUSTRATED BY
D. LINN WHORLEY

PRAYERS FOR CHILDREN
Bedtime & Otherwise!

TinyDon Publications®
Indianapolis, Indiana

A TinyDon Book

Copyright © 2020 by D. Linn Whorley

All rights reserved. This book may not be reproduced or transmitted in any form or by any means, electronic or mechanical, including photocopying, recording, or any information storage and retrieval system, without prior written permission of the publisher, except in the case of brief quotations embodied in articles or reviews.

Library of Congress Control Number: 2020913761
Whorley, D. Linn, 1964 -
Prayers for Children, Bedtime & Otherwise!
Spirit Food Series - Volume 1

Published by TinyDon Publications®, Indianapolis, Indiana.

For more information and resources, please visit us on the web at:
www.OneChild1.com

Book cover, logo and design by D. Linn Whorley
Written and edited by D. Linn Whorley

Identifiers: LCCN 2020913761 | ISBN 978-0-9839310-8-9

Publication Date: August 15, 2020

Printed and bound in the United States of America

This Book Belongs to _____

Thank you God, for this book of prayers.
It teaches me to talk to you everywhere.
It's a special book, made just for me,
that can teach me to know you the way you know me.
I can learn how to love and treat others too,
especially when they are sad and blue.
My new book of prayers can teach me so much
and I can even learn to feel your loving touch.
Thank you for my family too,
because they love me as much as I love you.
I know you have a special plan for me and I love you,
because you first loved me.

Family Morning Prayer

Dear Lord, thank you for waking us up today.
For all that you do to make our world ok.
We love you and need you to be with us
this day as we go to work and school and play.
Please help us to help someone in need today.
We love you God more than words can say.

To Know You

Lord help me to know and be like you.
Help me to see the good in people too
and help me to live a life that's pleasing to you.
Please help me to listen and hear your voice clear
and to always know that you are near.
For this I say and I pray,
every day and in every way.

Friends

Thank you Lord for my friends so dear.
Every friend both far and near.
My Friends are my friends all the day long,
as we dance and play and sing happy songs.
Each new day brings fun and adventure,
as we play and pretend together as friends.
We help each other when we are blue.
Without you God, we wouldn't know to do.

Pets and Animals

Thank you Lord for our pets
and other animals too.
Some live with us at our home
and some live in the zoo.
They make us laugh and smile each day.
Please keep them safe and warm we pray.

For Fun

Thank you Lord for the gift of fun.
To enjoy each day as we laugh and run.
Please help us to find joy in all we do,
Even as we do chores and homework too.
Please help mom and dad have fun today
and even find time with us to play.

Learning

Thank you God that I can learn
everything I need to know,
to help me live and love and grow.
Each day I pray to learn something new
and teach others too—even at school.

Our Home

Dear God, thank you for our home
that's cozy and warm.
It keeps us safe and dry, even in a storm.
Thank you for our family that I love so much,
even when we are apart,
we always stay in touch.
Some of us are near and some of us are far.
We are blessed each day, wherever we are.

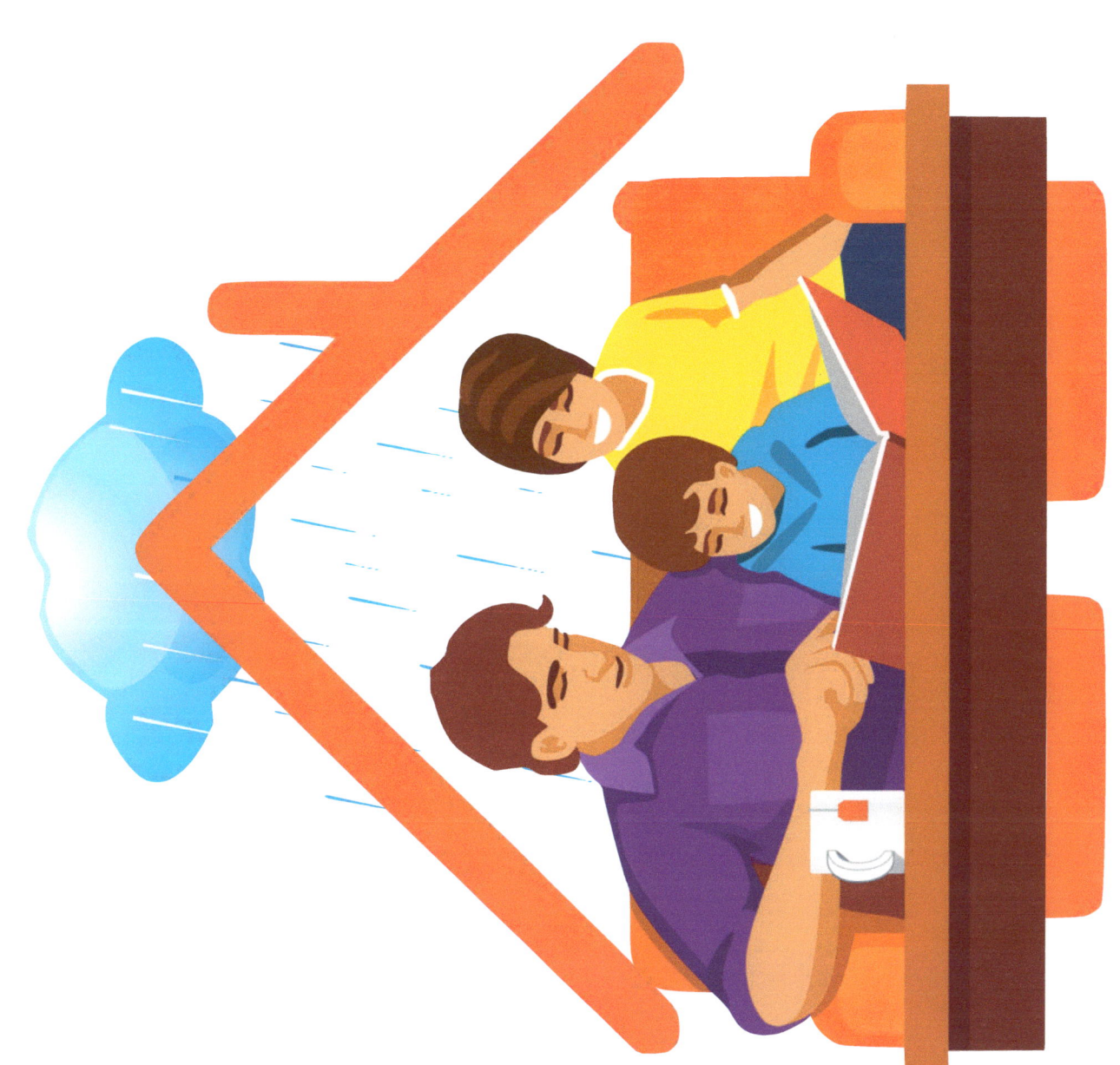

Bedtime Prayer

Thank you Lord for each new day,
and guiding my steps along the way.
Please keep me safe as I sleep all night
and watch over my family as they sleep tight,
and wake us up with your morning light.
In Jesus' Name I pray tonight—Amen.

Blessings

I'm thankful for the blessings I see.
Each day you grant grace and mercy for free.
I can enjoy the sun, flowers and skies of blue
and my family, my home and my freedom too.
In life I know I will succeed,
for you have given me all I need.

Hello Lord

Hello Lord and thank you for today.
Please give us the best start along our way.
Help us to do good and want to do right,
and not do bad so we can shine your light.
We know you are with us throughout our day,
and with us we pray you'll always stay.

Grace Before We Eat

Thank you Lord for the food we eat,
that fuels our bodies from our head to our feet.
Our meals make us healthy and strong
and carry us through the day so long.
Lord we pray now for those without,
please bless them the same,
in Jesus' Name.

Holidays

Thank you Lord for the holidays we share,
they bring us together and show we care.
We are blessed to give presents
and eat lots of food too,
for that we are thankful all because of you.

Prayer for Forgiveness

Lord forgive me for the things I may do,
that I soon find out are not like you.
Always help me to choose right instead of wrong.
I want to be kind and pleasing to you,
in everything I say and do.

Prayer When I Am Sad

Dear Lord, whenever I am sad
and I don't know what to do,
I try to never worry,
and remember to call on you.
I know you are always there
and I know you will always care.

Prayer for Sick Children

Lord bless the sick children in our world,
every little boy and girl.
Help them to know that you love them too
and give them faith to be
healed as good as new.

Prayer for Our Helpers

Thank you for our firemen
and our doctors and others too.
They work to save us everyday,
with help that comes from you.
Please give them strength and hope today
and guide them along their way, I pray.

Prayer for Our Military

Dear Lord, we pray for our Soldiers so dear,
to protect our country far and near.
Our Navy, Marines and Airmen too,
they all took an oath to volunteer it's true,
to defend our country with help from you.
Please keep them safe each and every day
and return them home to their families I pray.

Prayer for Our Leaders

Lord thank you for the leaders we trust,
to care for our country and people they must.
Please show them and teach them what to do,
and give them faith to believe in you.

Dear God,

All these prayers we ask in the name of your son—Jesus.

Amen.

ABOUT THE AUTHOR

D. Linn Whorley is a retired U.S. Army Non-commissioned Officer and the Author of *What I Want my Child to Know . . . A Mother's Loving Advice*. A devout Christian with a passion for Child Development & Teen Guidance, she is an empty nester and lives with her husband and toy poodle in Indianapolis, Indiana. For more information and resources visit OneChild1.com